Outdoor Sports
SKILLS

# HOW TO
# HIKE
# LIKE A PRO

## ASHLEY P. WATSON NORRIS

**Library of Congress Cataloging-in-Publication Data**
Norris, Ashley P. Watson.
    How to hike like a pro / Ashley P. Watson Norris.
        pages cm. — (Outdoor Sports Skills)
    Includes bibliographical references and index.
    Summary: "In this 'How-to' guide, learn the basic skills of hiking including how to pick a route, how to pack and dress appropriately, and what might be encountered while on a hike"—Provided by publisher.
    ISBN 978-1-62285-138-6
    1. Hiking—Handbooks, manuals, etc.—Juvenile literature. I. Title.
GV199.5.N67 2015
796.51—dc23
                        2013040803
Future editions:
Paperback ISBN: 978-1-62285-139-3        Single-User PDF ISBN: 978-1-62285-142-3
EPUB ISBN: 978-1-62285-141-6            Multi-User PDF ISBN: 978-1-62285-171-3

Printed in the United States of America
052014 Lake Book Manufacturing, Inc., Melrose Park, IL
10 9 8 7 6 5 4 3 2 1

**To Our Readers:** We have done our best to make sure all Internet addresses in this book were active and appropriate when we went to press. However, the author and the publisher have no control over and assume no liability for the material available on those Internet sites or on other Web sites they may link to. Any comments or suggestions can be sent by e-mail to comments@speedingstar.com or to the address below:

Speeding Star
Box 398, 40 Industrial Road
Berkeley Heights, NJ 07922
USA
www.speedingstar.com

Enslow Publishers, Inc., is committed to printing our books on recycled paper. The paper in every book contains 10% to 30% post-consumer waste (PCW). The cover board on the outside of each book contains 100% PCW. Our goal is to do our part to help young people and the environment too!

**Illustration Credits:** Shutterstock: (©Paul Staniszewski, p. 4; ©Jody, p. 5; ©Mikhail Olykainen, p. 6; ©Blend Images, p. 7; ©Spectruminfo, p. 8; ©Goodluz, p. 11(top); ©My Good Images, p. 11(bottom); ©rayjunk, p. 12; ©Annotee, p. 13; ©IgorXIII, p. 14; ©Lusoimages, p. 17; ©bogdan ionescu, p. 20; ©filip Robert, p. 21; ©Vronska, p. 24; ©Yeko Photo Studio, p. 25; ©Iasha, p. 26; visceralimage, p. 29; ©Martin Hladky, p. 30; ©Perutskyi Petro, p. 31; ©Steve Brigman, p. 32; ©Jane McIlroy, p. 33; ©PHOTOCREO Michal Bednarek, p. 35; ©maga, p. 36; ©Richard Pinder, p. 39; ©Peter Zaharov, p. 41; ©Zack Frank, p. 42; ©Larry Mundy, p. 43; ©Micha Klootwijk, p. 45). ©Thinkstock: (Jupiterimages/ Stockbyte, p. 15; DanBarnesCollection/iStock, p. 19; lzfCollection/iStock, 37).

**Cover Illustration:** ©Shutterstock/auremar

# CONTENTS

# FUNDAMENTALS

**Imagine walking on a dirt trail,** you hear something large in the trees up ahead. You walk into a clearing and see a herd of elk. The males are nine feet tall, have huge antlers, and look strong and made to run. They glance up at you and neither of you move. After several moments they decide that you and your family aren't a threat and they go back to grazing. You watch them for several minutes and take lots of photos.

As you continue your hike you scramble over large rocks, cross a small stream, walk through an aspen grove, and keep hiking uphill. After another hour you reach the mountain top, or summit. You step up to the cliff and enjoy the view. You can see miles and miles of forest and even your house from up here. A red-tailed hawk

*Elk are just one of many animals that can be encountered on a regular nature hike.*

*A hiker rests at Outlook Point, Yosemite National Park, California.*

flies by and lands on a tree below you. You're up super high!

At the summit you relax, drink some water, and enjoy the snacks you packed. As you start your hike back down you see that the elk are gone. But where they were you see a bunch of dark brown pebbles in a pile. After looking at your guidebook you figure out that it's elk scat, or poop.

When you finally reach the car you're tired but happy. It was a beautiful day to hike. You start planning your next hike to explore a different area, maybe a canyon, beach, or valley.

*Trails within the mountains can sometimes be clear like this one, or sometimes they can be covered with much more debris.*

## WHAT IS HIKING?

Walking long distances for fun and exercise is called hiking. It is a sport and an adventure and can be as simple or as difficult as you choose. The path you follow can be flat, steep, or hilly. You can hike on roads, a dirt trail, or make your own trail in the forest or desert.

**6**

There is no set length of time required because hiking is about having fun. Some people hike for just a few hours and carry water, snacks, and a jacket. Other people hike for days and will carry big packs with tents, sleeping bags, lots of food, and even a book or two to read.

Find out what style of hiking you enjoy the most. Go hiking with a friend, a parent, or a hiking group. It's a great way to have fun and see wild animals, beautiful scenery, and get into nature.

*Hiking with friends is a fun activity.*

## ETIQUETTE

Hiking etiquette is the informal guidelines that lets all hikers enjoy the trail and nature but with no negative impact. Following etiquette means that the trail and wildlife will be there to see and enjoy in the future.

A popular saying amongst hikers and nature groups is: take nothing but pictures and leave nothing but footprints. It means the only thing you should take

*Most trails won't have garbage cans along the way, so it is always important to bring something in which you can carry your garbage until you can dispose of trash the right way.*

while hiking is photos. Leave what you find where you found it. Don't take any shells, rocks, plants, or animals with you. The only thing you should leave behind are footprints. This means that no trash should be left behind, even biodegradable food items such as apple cores and banana peels.

Uphill hikers have the right of way. If you're hiking downhill and meet hikers that are going uphill, then you should step off the path to allow them to pass. When you take a break move to the side of the trail so other hikers can pass you.

During long hikes you will probably need to use the bathroom. Pick an area more than two hundred feet away from water, the trail, and campgrounds. This will ensure that the water stays clean and that you will have privacy.

To urinate, choose a bare spot with no grass, plants, or trees. For solid human waste, or feces, dig an eight-inch-deep hole, called a cat hole, and use that as a toilet. When you're done, cover it up with dirt but don't pack the soil down. This will allow the feces, or poop, to decompose. Toilet paper takes years to decompose, so it should be put in a plastic bag and packed out.

## PICKING A ROUTE

A hike can be whatever you want. Pick the best hike for the time you have and your group's skill level. Find your options by talking to other hikers, look for hiking books, maps, and Web sites that list hikes for your area.

First decide how difficult of a hike you want. Most hiking guides separate hikes into three categories: easy, moderate, or difficult. These categories account for distance, elevation, or vertical height climbed, and the trail type.

Next decide who will be hiking. The group must go at the speed of the slowest hiker and cannot leave a member behind. The route selected must be suitable for every hiker participating.

Figure out if you want to hike for a few hours or a few days. Then determine what hiking trails in the area match what you want.

One-way trails are also common They have a final destination and then the hikers must turn around and go back the same way they came.

Study the maps or trail guides for the area you plan to hike. Those maps will help you decide where you want to start, take breaks, and the final destination of your hike.

# NAVIGATION

Maps contain a lot of important information. For every hike there is an appropriate map. A trail map is all that is necessary for hiking well-used trails. It will show where to start hiking, areas of interest, distances, buildings, and roads.

For hiking off-trail you will need a topographical (*to-po-graph-i-cal*) map. Topographical maps allow hikers to see the shape of the land on a map. These specialized maps have lots of lines called contour lines. Contour lines connect many points of the same elevation. If you walked along a contour line you would not go higher or lower. The farther apart the lines are, the flatter the

*This hiker is prepared for a hike through the Himalaya Mountains.*

area is. The closer the lines are, the steeper the area is. Topographical maps also show other important features like railroads, mines, bridges, buildings, water, campgrounds, trails, and roads.

Many hikers use a compass to figure out which direction they are going. A compass has a rotating arrow and a base plate that is marked North, South, East, and West. To find North, line up the moving arrow with the word North, or "N." It has lines that mark all

*A compass is a good tool to have because it can tell in which direction you are facing or moving.*

## PRO TIPS AND TRICKS

An altimeter is a handheld gadget that tells you your elevation. You can use your topographic map and altimeter to find the exact contour line that marks where you are on the map.

*While most smartphones now come with GPS capabilities built in, many hikers prefer to use an actual handheld GPS for more accurate information.*

360 degrees in a circle so that you can go in a more exact direction.

A Global Positioning System, or GPS, is an electronic, handheld device that sends a signal to satellites in outer space to pinpoint your exact location. Some smart phones can be used as a GPS device. This is another way to find where you are and which way you should hike. Make sure your GPS is fully charged before leaving home and ensure you know how to operate it.

## TRAIL FITNESS

Hiking is different from walking around your house, school, or in a store. While hiking you need to concentrate on your feet: where they land, how they hit the ground, and how fast they move.

Take careful steps and know exactly where you are putting your feet so you don't trip, slip, or fall. When hiking uphill, downhill, or in rough areas, take shorter steps and land flat-footed. This way you will be less likely to fall and hurt your ankle or foot.

### DID YOU KNOW?

You burn over 300 calories an hour while hiking.

*To ensure you can handle carrying the heavy gear needed on a hike, prepare by first taking a shorter hike. The result will tell you if you can handle a longer, tougher hike.*

# PRO TIPS AND TRICKS

The best way to prepare for a hike is to practice! Take short hikes with the pack and in the clothes and shoes you'll be wearing.

*Some hikers use walking sticks such as these to help them keep their balance, as well as a way to remind them to watch where they are walking.*

It's important to pace yourself, or walk at a steady speed. The right pace lets you walk and talk easily. It's a good idea to take several rest breaks along the way. It's a chance to talk, enjoy the scenery, eat a snack, and drink water. Hiking is not a race, and the pace should be set by the slowest person in the group.

Stretching is an important part of any sport and prevents pulled muscles and injuries. Hiking uses lots of leg, back, and shoulder muscles to carry you and your pack to new and exciting places. Stretch your upper and lower legs, ankles, back, and shoulders well before and after the hike. This will prevent muscles from being sore or cramping up on the trail.

# FIRST AID

Every hiker should have a first aid kit with them and know how to use it. A good first aid kit is small, lightweight, and compact but has everything needed for a hiking emergency. It should contain: big and small bandages, ointment, sunscreen, gauze, medical tape, scissors, tweezers, triangular bandage cloth, sterile cotton pads, blister supplies, medicines, and any personal prescriptions.

One of the most common injuries from hiking is blisters. Blisters are caused by shoes or socks that don't fit correctly. They rub against your foot, causing fluid to form under the skin; it can be very painful. Treat a blister by putting a thick bandage over it called a moleskin. Center the hole in the moleskin on the blister and put the sticky side on your skin. If the blister has broken open, put ointment on it. Then cover the entire site with medical tape to hold the moleskin in place.

Other common hiking injuries are scrapes, cuts, insect stings or bites, reactions to poisonous plants, and sunburn. These injuries are usually minor and can be treated with the proper items in a basic first aid kit. Treat any injuries immediately so they don't get worse.

Many hospitals, schools, and organizations offer first aid classes. The skills learned in these classes are good things to know on and off the trail.

*A good first aid kit has the basic supplies in case of emergency.*

## DID YOU KNOW?

You can prevent blisters by wearing shoes and socks that fit well and by not wearing new shoes on a long hike.

## HIKING PLANS

A hiking plan is very important and should be made for every hike. Hiking plans describe exactly where you are going, when you are leaving, who is going, how long you will be gone, and when you plan to be back. It should include as many details as possible because it will be used to find you if you don't return at the set time you were expected.

Hiking plans are left with somebody you trust who is not participating in the hike. If you become lost, injured, or don't return on time, then others will use your hiking plan to find you. This means that you must stick to your hiking plan. Then once you finish your hike, contact the person with your plan so they know you are safe and had a successful hike.

For well-known hikes it is OK to use the approximate hiking time listed in guidebooks and maps. For off-trail hiking a good rule-of-thumb is that adults hike 2-3 miles an hour and children hike 1-2 miles per hour on flat ground. Hiking uphill takes more time than across flat ground. For every 1,000 feet in elevation you climb, add

## PRO TIPS AND TRICKS

After hiking in thick woods check your groin, armpits, behind your knees, and neck, for tiny bloodsucking insects called ticks. If you find one, tell an adult immediately.

*If you get lost, the most important thing is to remain calm and look to see if you remember seeing any significant landmarks.*

an hour to the hiking time. This will make up for extra rest breaks and slower walking speeds.

## WHAT TO DO IF LOST

Even the best hiker can get distracted and find themselves lost. If you are lost, don't panic. Retrace your steps to your last known location on the map or trail, if possible. If not, look at your map and try to figure out exactly where you are. Look for large or unmoving features such as buildings, mountaintops, lakes, or streams. Try to find those on your map and figure out exactly where you are on the map and where you need to go.

If you can't figure out where you are, then don't move. Stay where you are. When you are late returning, the people who have your hiking plan will start looking for you. While you wait, try to make yourself visible by using items you're wearing, in your pack, or in the area. Put on a brightly colored jacket or hat. Use rocks or branches in a clearing to make an X or an arrow pointing to where you are. Spell out S-O-S, a signal of distress.

Three signals of anything usually means distress, or that somebody needs help. Use your whistle to let others know you need help by blowing three short blasts. At night flash your flashlight three times. Raising both arms above your head and waving them is another great way to signal to others that you need help.

*Having a large backpack doesn't mean that it has to weigh a lot. But it gives the option of taking along a few extra supplies.*

**20**

## GEAR

Hiking gear can make the journey more fun and keep you comfortable. If you take too much stuff, then your pack will be heavy, you'll be tired, sore, and won't have fun. Pack what you need, a few emergency supplies, and nothing extra.

The pack you use should be large enough to carry what you need for the hike, but not so large that there is a lot of extra space. Packs come in different

*This illustration shows many of the basic, yet necessary gear to take on a hike.*

shapes, sizes, and fits and are designed for people of all shapes and sizes. Make sure you use a pack that fits you well.

Hiking poles or sticks can help you keep your balance and pace. Poles let you use both your arms and legs as you hike uphill. Most poles are adjustable; make them shorter when going uphill and longer when going downhill. Use a natural arm swing, keep your forearms at the same angle as the ground and place your poles on firm ground.

Make sure you pack a cell phone, camera, field guide, map, compass or GPS, first aid kit, camera, sunscreen, magnifying glass, flashlight, small knife or multi-tool, water, hand sanitizer, snacks, a plastic bag to pack out trash, and warm or cold weather clothes.

For long and overnight hikes a few more items will be needed. You'll need a small shovel to dig a cat hole, toilet paper, and food. You may need a water filtration system and fire starting kit. If you're spending the night you'll need a sleeping bag, tent, toothbrush, toothpaste, extra socks, and underwear.

## PRO TIPS AND TRICKS

Your skin can get sunburn on sunny days, cloudy days, and from the reflection off snow. Protect your skin by wearing long sleeves and pants and sunscreen. Protect your eyes from the sun by wearing sunglasses.

# CLOTHES

Dress like an onion. Wear lots of layers that you can take off when you're hot and put back on when you're cold. Hiking clothes should be very comfortable, loose fitting, and thin.

Clothes have been designed specifically for hikers. Some clothes have built-in bug repellent to keep away bugs. Others protect your skin from sunburn. Some hiking pants have legs that zip off and turn into shorts.

Hiking in the summer can get really hot, so follow the Australian hiking slogan, "Slip, Slop, Slap." Slip on a long-sleeved shirt, slop on the sunscreen, and slap on a hat to protect yourself from the sun.

On mountain hikes remember to pack a jacket, gloves, and hat to protect you from the wind, rain, or snow. Dressing in layers will help you be warm at the top of a mountain where it can be cold even in the middle of summer.

Hiking shoes should be comfortable and fit well, not too big or too small. Hiking shoes are made for different types of weather and hiking conditions such as hot, cold, and wet. Choose the shoe that is best suited for your style of hiking and where you like to hike. Try on new hiking shoes with the same socks that you plan to hike in. Wear them around the house and on short hikes to break them in. This will prevent blisters and sore feet after a long day of hiking.

*Dressing in layers is important because you can always take clothing off. However, you can't put clothing on that you don't have, so it's better to overdress than to under dress.*

# FOOD

Hiking requires a lot of energy, so you will probably get hungry during your hike. Pack several different types of snacks that you can eat.

Many hikers prefer a nut and dried fruit mix called trail mix or GORP. GORP stands for Good Old Raisins and Peanuts. It provides lots of energy and can be eaten while hiking. You can mix your favorite nuts and fruits together or you can buy it premixed.

Granola bars, cookies, fruits, and veggies are another good snack option for hikes. Celery sticks filled with peanut butter and raisins, carrots, bananas, berries, oranges, and apples are good too. Be sure to pack

*Trail mix is the perfect snack to take along on a hike.*

something that you like to eat and that will travel well. Just make sure you pack out any leftover parts such as apple cores, banana or orange peels, and wrappers.

Pack healthy food and snacks. They are best for you, and most of them don't need to be kept cold. They can be eaten while hiking. So don't bring soft drinks, instead bring water. If you bring your own water, you know that you have a safe reliable source of water. Leave the candy bars at home and instead bring dried fruit and nuts (with a bit of chocolate). Healthy snacks are the best food for the trail.

*Water bottles or canteens, like the one shown, are important to have while hiking to prevent from becoming dehydrated.*

# WATER

When you are hiking you will get thirsty and need to drink water. This will replace the water your body is losing through sweat. When you're hiking hard, you can lose one to two liters of water in sweat in an hour.

If you don't drink enough water you will become dehydrated. Signs of dehydration are: dark yellow urine, headache, loss of energy, fast heartbeat, and thirst. This can be a serious life-threatening condition if ignored. Make sure you drink water even if you're not thirsty throughout the hike. If you're thirsty, then drink until you're not.

There are many ways to efficiently carry water while hiking. One of the easiest is by carrying a water bottle. Water bottles come in many sizes and shapes. Some can even hold boiling water, which makes fixing meals easier. Many hiking packs have spots designed to hold water bottles.

Hydration packs are designed to hold large amounts of water and are usually worn as a backpack. They have a tube that comes over the shoulder of the strap and hangs down the front. You suck on the end of it like a straw. These come in many shapes and sizes and the larger ones have extra pockets.

Longer hikes will require you to get water from rivers, streams, ponds, or lakes. This water must be treated so that you won't get sick from the microscopic bugs and germs in the water. You can purify the water with iodine or chlorine tablets, filters, or by boiling the water for two to three minutes.

# IN THE WILD

## ANIMALS

Mountain lions, foxes, and bears, oh my!

One of the most exciting things about hiking is seeing the wildlife in their natural environment. Keep your eyes open, be quiet, and you will probably see wild animals. Wildlife does not benefit from human interaction, so keep a safe distance between you and them. Respect the animals and their habitat by not disturbing them.

Don't feed them because human food isn't good for animals, and it isn't part of their normal diet. Wild animals can carry bugs and diseases that can be passed along to humans. Keep a safe distance, and if you get bitten by an animal tell an adult immediately.

As you hike you will probably see animal tracks or footprints. Each animal has a distinctive set of tracks. With practice and a good field guide you can identify the animals that made the tracks.

## PRO TIPS AND TRICKS

Snakes bite if they feel threatened. If you see one don't touch it, even if it is dead. Snakes have reflexes that act automatically; they can strike and inject venom several hours after they die.

One animal that can be encountered while hiking in the woods is the mountain lion. Make sure to keep a safe distance from all animals, especially this one.

*The most common scat that will probably be found during a hike will be deer scat.*

Another sign that animals leave behind is scat, feces, or poop. Look carefully at the scat but don't touch it with your hands. Use a stick. See if you can tell what the animal ate and guess what type of animal it came from. Ask these questions to try to figure out what animal left the scat:

- Is it big or small?
- What color is it?
- What is it shaped like? A ball, a Tootsie Roll, or a log?
- Does it have round, flat or pointy ends?
- How many droppings are there, one or many?

- Is there anything in the scat like fur or seeds?
- What kind of animals live in the area?

# PLANTS

Our ancestors survived by eating what they found growing wild. There are many nutritious and delicious plants, berries, seeds, roots, flowers, and leaves. However, you must know exactly what is and is not edible. Use a field guide to identify and then show anything to an adult before you eat it. Many plants cause rashes, upset stomachs, or can be deadly.

## DID YOU KNOW?

If you're feeling brave, pick the purple fruit off of a prickly pear cactus. Peel off the skin and eat the inner fruit; it tastes like sweet bubble gum and watermelon flavored candy.

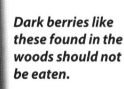

*Dark berries like these found in the woods should not be eaten.*

Plants growing along a tree like this may seem harmless. But this is poison ivy, and as the name suggests, is poisonous.

If in doubt, don't eat it. Eat the food you brought.

Dandelion, hibiscus, daylily, and chamomile flowers are edible and can be eaten in a variety of ways. While dandelion stems are not edible, dandelion leaves are and have a bitter taste. Wash them off with drinking water to make a salad.

Touching some plants will cause itchy rashes and should be avoided. Poison ivy, poison oak, and poison sumac are three poisonous plants. Make sure you know what their leaves look like so if you see them you can stay away. If you do accidentally touch them, don't scratch. Wash off your skin with just water and put on anti-itch medicine, like calamine lotion.

These rhymes will help you remember what to avoid.

- Leaves of three, let it be. Side leaflets like mittens will itch like the dickens. Hairy vine, no friend of mine. (poison ivy)
- White and yellow, kill a fellow. Purple and blue, good for you. Red, could be good, could be dead. (berries)
- If it ain't hollow, don't swallow; if it's reddish, you could be deadish. (mushrooms)

## TERRAIN

While you're hiking you will walk over and through many different types of land features, called terrain. Impress your family and friends by identifying them on a topographical map and during your hike.

A hill or summit is a high point that

*Hiking through a valley can be relaxing because it is usually flatter ground and the view can be great too!*

is surrounded by ground that slopes down in all directions. On a topographical map look for a small circle. That is the top of the hill.

A valley is a long area that is lower than the surrounding terrain. Valleys usually have rivers running through them. They can be narrow or quite flat and wide. On your map look for an area where the contour lines seem to meet from opposite sides. Usually there is a road, river, or flat area with less contour lines in the middle.

Low ground is called a depression. These are easy to spot on the map because of the circular contour lines with tick marks on them. The tick marks are pointing towards the depression.

An area with a vertical drop is called a cliff. Cliffs also have tick marks on them but if you look carefully several contour lines have merged into one. The tick marks also point towards one side only, where the ground drops drastically.

Switchbacks are on the sides of steep hills or mountains. These trails cut back and forth in a 'z' pattern. They require less energy than going straight up the mountain and cause less erosion.

# WEATHER

Hiking in sunny weather with the right clothes is more fun than hiking in rain or snow with no jacket. Before a hike, make sure you know what the weather will be by checking the weather forecast for the area where you will be hiking. Dress like you're an onion, in multiple layers, to keep warm or stay cool during your hike.

## DID YOU KNOW?

The water in lakes, streams, ponds, and rivers could make you really sick. Treat all water before you drink it.

*Dressing like an onion comes in handy when you are at the summit and rain clouds start to roll in.*

*Big cumulonimbus clouds like these are usually a sign of bad weather to come.*

Take into account that it is colder and more windy at the top of a mountain than at the base. A good rule of thumb is that for every 1,000 feet you hike up in elevation, the temperature will drop 3-5 degrees Fahrenheit.

Wind is affected by mountains, valleys, trees, and the temperature. The terrain will funnel or block the wind, so expect to walk through windy areas during your hike. If you are hiking up a mountain, once you pass the tree line there will be no trees to block the wind, so expect more wind.

There are many different types of clouds, but the one hikers should be wary of is cumulonimbus (pronounced cu-mu-lo-nimbus) clouds. These are fluffy clouds that are very tall and are shaped like mushrooms. These clouds bring thunder, lightning, and severe weather with them.

If you're caught in a lightning storm, don't panic. Find an area away from water, tall cliffs, and solitary trees. Sit on a blanket, sleeping pad, or backpack with your feet drawn up close to your body.

*While some bad weather might be unexpected, with the proper planning there is no reason that hikers cannot select the perfect day to go hiking.*

**37**

## GEOCACHING

Geocaching is fun to do on a hike. It's a type of treasure hunting. You use a GPS to find a set of coordinates. At these coordinates are hidden caches or treasure. Each cache has a logbook, pencil, and a few treasures. Write your name and the date you found the cache in the logbook. Look through the treasures and if you see something you want, take it, but you must leave something of equal or greater value for the next person to find.

If you, a friend, or your parents have a GPS device or a smartphone you can geocache. It is a great way to explore your favorite hiking trail, campsite, or town. You can even make and register your own cache.

Many people make it into a group game and try to find more geocaches than another group. Others set up challenges like taking a silly photo, or doing an activity like kissing a metal horse. You may even find a travel bug or geocoin. These treasures can be tracked online and you can see the places they have traveled around the world.

## DID YOU KNOW?

There are about 900,000 caches in North America.

# PRO TIPS AND TRICKS

If you can't see landmarks or the trail because of bad weather such as fog, rain, or snow then your best option may be to wait where you are until the weather improves.

*Geocaching can make hiking more fun. Reading the logbook will show how many different hikers participated, and all the different parts of the world that they came from.*

## DID YOU KNOW?

John Muir was one of America's most important conservationists. He was a cofounder of the Sierra Club, which has established numerous national parks, and currently has over 1.3 million members.

There are many Web sites dedicated to geocaching. They have lists of caches and you can search for ones in your campsite or along your hike.

## FAMOUS TRAILS & FAMOUS HIKERS

The most famous hiking trail in the United States is the Appalachian Trail. It goes through fourteen states and is 2,180 miles long. There are hundreds of hikes along the Appalachian Trail that offer short easy hikes, one or two day-long trips, and tough week-long hikes.

Some people try to hike the entire Appalachian Trail at once; they are called thru-hikers. Thru-hikers usually start in Georgia in the spring and finish in Maine about six months later. In 2011 Jennifer Pharr Davis set the unofficial record for the fastest thru-hike of the Appalachian Trail. She finished in 46 days instead of 180 like most hikers. Jennifer hiked fifteen to eighteen hours every day. That means she hiked 47 miles every day for 46 days!

Mt. Whitney is the highest mountain in the lower United States. In 2011, then seven-year-old Tyler Armstrong became the youngest person known to hike Mount Whitney. It's peak is 14,505 feet above sea level. He got to the summit, in less than eight hours! In 2012, Tyler became the second youngest person to hike Africa's highest mountain, Mount Kilimanjaro, which is 19,341 feet above sea level.

There are 398 National Parks and over 7,000 state parks in the United States with thousands of great hiking trails. Find parks near you and explore their hiking trails.

*This is the sign that is found at the top of Mt. Kilimanjaro.*

# CONSERVATION

Conservation is preserving or preventing the waste or loss of nature, wildlife, and trails. They need to be conserved so that many people can enjoy them. There are many ways you can help conserve nature and hiking trails.

You can do this as you hike by picking up trash left by others. If you see something where it shouldn't be, like a log laying across the trail, write down where it was and report it to the group or organization who maintains the trail.

*One of the most well-known National Parks in the world is Yellowstone National Park.*

PLEASE BRING YOUR TRASH AND GARBAGE BACK WITH YOU. HELP US KEEP YOUR LAND CLEAN.

*It's hard to believe that people wouldn't throw their garbage out on their own, but conservation groups have to put up signs like this to remind visitors that nature isn't their garbage can.*

Another simple way to preserve the trail is by staying on it. Don't use or make a cutoff. Cutoffs are usually found near the turn in switchbacks. Cutoffs were made by hikers who didn't want to go all the way to the turn. They wanted to cut off part of the trail. Unfortunately, cutoffs damage the trail and the landscape by causing erosion. Respect the trail and don't use cutoffs.

There are many conservation groups out there that protect and keep the trails in good shape for hikers.

They are mostly made up of volunteers who do a variety of things from maintain Web sites, enter data, improve or fix trails and facilities, and teach others about hiking etiquette, conservation, and more. Find a local group and do your part to protect your favorite trails, animals, and campsites.

# SEARCH & RESCUE

Unfortunately, many people get injured or lost in the wilderness and need to be rescued. There are specially trained mountain rescue organizations all over the world. These highly trained teams find and help people in the wilderness. They regularly use helicopters, horses, boats, or snowmobiles to get to and from distant locations.

These groups contain people with specialized medical knowledge, extensive climbing, hiking, fire or police training, and mountain rescue knowledge. Some rescuers are forest rangers but many of them are volunteers.

Some mountain rescue teams have search dogs. These dogs use their outstanding sense of smell to follow a person's scent. When they're working they wear a vest or harness, and sometimes they wear booties to protect their feet.

These highly trained dogs are chosen as puppies and begin their training when they're seven or eight weeks old. Common breeds used for rescue units are German shepherds, golden retrievers, and Labrador retrievers. They have to pass a series of tests before they become certified and can go on an actual rescue mission.

## DID YOU KNOW?

The U.S. Air Force has a job called Pararescue. These Paramedics undergo some of the toughest military training so that they can rescue people from land and sea in both peace and combat situations.

*Seeing a Search and Rescue (S&R) helicopter is usually the sign of a lost hiker. Or, one who has been found!*

Both human and dog search-and-rescue members must be in excellent shape and enjoy being outdoors in all types of weather conditions. Team members practice a lot in teams and individually. They risk their lives to find others who need help and spend hours or days looking for lost or injured people. They are true heroes.

# FURTHER READING

## BOOKS

Berger, Karen. *Be Prepared Hiking and Backpacking*. New York: DK Publishing, 2007.

Goldenberg, Marni and Bruce Martin, eds. *Hiking and Backpacking*. Champaign, Illinois: Human Kinetics, Inc., 2007.

McKinney, John. *Hiking*. North Mankato, MN: Cherry Lake Publishing, 2007.

*National Geographic Kids National Parks Guide U.S.A.* Edited by National Geographic Editors. Washington, D.C.: 2012.

Skurka, Andrew. *The Ultimate Hiker's Gear Guide: Tools & Techniques to Hit the Trail*. Washington, D.C. National Geographic, 2012.

Stevenson, Jason. *The Complete Idiot's Guide to Backpacking and Hiking*. New York: Penguin Group, 2010.

## INTERNET ADDRESSES

### National Park Service
<www.nps.gov>

### State Parks
<www.americasstateparks.org>

### American Hiking Society
<www.americanhiking.org>

### Geocaching
<www.geocaching.com>

# INDEX